*Afri*FLUENCE

UNLOCKING THE POTENTIAL OF AFRICAN INFLUENCERS

By Emmanuel Bope and Solange Bope

CANADA

PAN AFRICAN LIFESTYLE INC.

Authors: Emmanuel Bope and Solange Bope

Printed and bound in Canada

First printing Marh 2023

Published by PAN AFRICAN LIFESTYLE Inc.

Calgary, Alberta

ISBN 978-1-7776963-9-9 Paperback
ISBN 978-1-7776963-4-4 eBook

www.panafricanlifestyle.com

A portion of the proceeds from this book is allocated to empower African creatives through initiatives by Pan African Lifestyle Inc. Thank you for supporting Afrifluencers in the motherland.

DEDICATION

In the motherland resides a remarkable people, unlike any other. They are the architects of dreams, the custodians of vision—the ones who perceive the world through a kaleidoscope of possibilities. Often dismissed and underestimated, they stand undeterred, defying the shackles of conventional wisdom that dare to dim Africa's brilliance.

In the swirling media vortex of doubt, fear-mongering, division, and misunderstanding, they remain steadfast, their hearts beating in unison with the pulse of The African Dream. Their influence cannot be denied, for they are the alchemists who transmute the raw essence of Africa into a tapestry of truth, hope, and wonder, painting vivid strokes of a new narrative upon the digital canvas of the world.

Armed with nothing but their imagination and boundless ambition, they forge bridges that span oceans, uniting Africa with its diaspora across distant horizons. Through the power of storytelling and creative ingenuity, they propel the continent forward, breathing life into the dreams of generations yet unborn. Though skeptics may scoff and cynics may sneer, their light shines as brightly as the African sun, illuminating The African Dream for all who dare to see.

Afrifluencers, this tome pays homage to your indomitable spirit and celebrates your creative genius. It is a clarion call to awaken your potential and unleash it for the greater good of Africa. As you delve into its pages, may you find inspiration, guidance, and the unwavering belief that within you lies the power to shape the destiny of a continent.

CONTENTS

DISCLAIMER

Before delving into the core of our discussion, let's anticipate and address any objections that skeptics may raise. Whether rooted in genuine skepticism or tinged with envy and disdain, we are prepared to confront them directly. However, let's clarify: Afrifluence is not a panacea for Africa's myriad challenges. We are not so naïve as to suggest that the continent's complex array of geopolitical, economic, structural, and societal issues can be resolved with a single solution.

Nevertheless, we are here to advocate for a different perspective—one that places agency firmly in the hands of the people. Humans are inherently emotional beings, drawn to ideas that resonate with their deepest aspirations. And who better to articulate these ideas and embed them in our collective consciousness than storytellers? Let it be clear: we deeply value the contributions of scientists, educators, engineers, and countless other professionals. Yet today, we choose to highlight a group often overlooked.

Within Africa's vast abundance of natural resources lies its most precious gem: the African mind. This reservoir of wisdom and innovation has shaped civilizations and propelled progress. Yet, it has been neglected and underestimated for far too long. It is time to harness the limitless creativity pulsating within the African mind—a creativity that holds the key to unlocking the continent's true potential.

MESSAGE

When we launched Pan African Lifestyle, optimism was our north star, yet the magnitude of what it became was beyond our wildest dreams. As creatives, we veered off the well-trodden path laid out by our well-meaning African parents, who envisioned futures for us in law or medicine, not in the uncertain world of creativity and innovation. The notion of making a living, let alone a difference, through creativity, marketing, and communication seemed like a distant fantasy. Yet, here we are.

The journey wasn't straightforward. College initially, then a pivot to online university offered us the flexibility and focus we needed to dive deep into marketing communication and branding. We had a string of entrepreneurial misfires and were on the verge of giving up when the pandemic of 2020 struck. It was then, in the quiet of a 1 AM brainstorm, that Pan African Lifestyle was born, never to look back.

Originally, our aim was modest: a Pan-African streetwear brand to make Pan-Africanism cool. But as our ambitions grew, so did our vision, evolving into a media company and lifestyle brand at the forefront of Afrocentrism, driven by the vibrant energies of Pan-African pop culture, fashion, and experiences. The explosive rise of Afrobeats and the influential power of African social media influencers to redirect the global gaze towards the continent was our clarion call. We were set on using creativity not just as an expression but as a tool for tangible change.

Our initial endeavor, "Live The African Dream," was a manifesto for the diaspora, outlining eight principles for re-rooting in the motherland. Yet, we recognized a missing piece: the transformative power of mindset, particularly through creativity. It dawned on us that creatives are the catalysts for change, the very essence that could ignite the Pan African Lifestyle, making The African Dream a reality for many.

Thus, we felt compelled to craft a guide centered around our first love: branding and marketing. This wasn't just about acknowledging the influence of creatives; it was about defining the essence of an African influencer—or

"Afrifluencer"—and showcasing how "Afrifluence" could revolutionize African tourism and entrepreneurship. It's about repatriation, bridging continents, and, crucially, rewriting the African narrative for generations to come.

Afrifluence is more than a guideline for creatives; it's a call to action, offering practical advice on leveraging social media and the art of documentation to build an authentic African brand. This brand isn't just a business; it's a movement, one that can shift perceptions, inspire new mindsets, and foster a creative revolution on the continent. This book is a beacon for Afrifluencers everywhere, urging them to embrace their creative prowess and understand the weight of influence they carry. In the uncharted territories of African social influence, we're not just participants; we're pioneers, determined to leave a legacy that echoes the true spirit of The African Dream.

Regards,

Emmanuel Bope and Solange Bope

STORY

With the inception of Pan African Lifestyle (PAL), our intention surpassed the mere establishment of another media entity. We embarked on a mission to champion Afrocentrism, serving as a guiding light for The African Dream. In the memorable summer of 2020, fueled by the pulsating beats of Afrobeats and the kaleidoscope of Afropop culture resonating across social platforms, an insistent call to innovate stirred within us. Our aspirations transcended conventional content creation; we aimed to craft a captivating narrative, cultivate a lifestyle, and spark a movement that would deeply resonate with individuals of African descent globally.

Our vision was both bold and lucid: to forge a brand that transcends the digital domain, offering not mere stories but immersive encounters—encompassing a spectrum from apparel and card games to literature and an Afropop anthem. With PAL, our objective was to kindle a flame within the African diaspora, nurturing a sense of unity, pride, and purpose that transcends borders. Witnessing PAL's evolution into a name reverberating throughout the Pan-African community has been profoundly exhilarating.

That summer served as a catalyst for a profound movement. Delving into the global influence of Afrobeats and Afropop, we unearthed an unprecedented opportunity. We aimed to establish a platform that would inspire a reconnection with African heritage and narrate an untold story in a manner befitting its significance. Within a short span, we transformed our vision into reality—introducing a product line that encapsulates the essence of the Pan African Lifestyle. Collaborating with influencers, pivotal figures capable of reshaping narratives, proved to be transformative. Their endorsement propelled PAL from a brand to a movement, embodying a collective embrace of The African Dream.

Our journey through social media has been nothing short of revolutionary. Our platforms flourished, amassing over 100K followers and generating millions of impressions, underscoring a global thirst for authentic African narratives. This surge of interest attracted a diverse array of creatives, content creators, and professionals, all eager to glean insights from our unique storytelling approach. This momentum spurred the development of "Afrifluence," a guide designed to empower African influencers—or Afrifluencers, as we affectionately dub them.

The enthusiastic response to this initiative underscored an urgent need for a fresh discourse on authentic African branding and content creation, one that embraces not only the continent but also the global diaspora. We are not merely recounting our story; we are issuing a clarion call, offering a blueprint for a new generation of Afrifluencers determined to leave their mark and shape Africa's future with their creative prowess.

PREFACE

Years before becoming known as Africa's most influential YouTuber, and arguably the top Afrifluencer across all platforms, Berthold Kobby Winkler Ackon, formerly identified as a self-proclaimed traditional village boy from Ghana, underwent a remarkable transformation on his journey to becoming a prominent figure in the realms of social media influence, international Pan-African advocacy, and esteemed social journalism. Raised in the Kofikrom region of western Ghana, Kobby imbibed essential values from his upbringing—humility, self-control, diligence, respect for the environment, and a zest for life.

His trajectory took a pivotal turn when he seized the opportunity to pursue higher education at Shenyang Aerospace University in China following the completion of his secondary education. Armed with a degree in aeronautical engineering, Kobby made a life-altering decision to forsake his conventional career path and channel his energy into freelancing as a YouTube vlogger. Initially skeptical, his father eventually suggested that if he were to proceed, he should aim to make an impact. Encouraged by his unwaveringly supportive mother, Kobby adopted the moniker Wode Maya for his newly launched YouTube channel, as a homage to his mother ("my mom" in Mandarin). Setting an ambitious goal of posting a video every day, Kobby initially focused on Chinese-African international relations. However, as his journey unfolded, he redirected his content towards inspiring the African diaspora to invest in their homelands and showcasing Africa to the world.

The turning point came with a viral post documenting his travels to Kigali, Rwanda, propelling Wode Maya to the pinnacle of African vlogging on YouTube. With over 1 million subscribers, 150 million views, and a growing audience, Wode Maya's impact reverberated so profoundly that even the CEO of YouTube acknowledged his remarkable achievements. Recognized as a trailblazer in reshaping the African narrative, Wode Maya receives commendation from many in the diaspora who credit him with inspiring their return to their respective countries. Serving as the epitome of the African Dream, his ongoing efforts with the "Africa to the World" campaign have redefined the landscape, encouraging African content producers to leverage social media in embracing and sharing the rich tapestry of the African story. Wode Maya stands as a beacon, illuminating the path for a new generation eager to contribute to the narrative of a thriving and dynamic Africa.

Wode Maya is the quintessential example of the power of the new African generation in this digital era. One doesn't need substantial capital to start, only the will, passion, and a unique African perspective or narrative. In the past, before the internet, people turned to the radio or television for entertainment after a long day. Today, the advent of smartphones, tablets, laptops, and streaming platforms like YouTube has revolutionized content consumption, making it more accessible and immediate. This shift presents an opportunity for Africans to reshape the narrative of the continent and build wealth through content creation and digital entrepreneurship.

While we await the day when Africa will be structurally, economically, and politically borderless, it is evident that Africa is digitally borderless now. This digital landscape presents a battleground where Africans can reclaim their narrative and build wealth for the continent. By dominating the digital space as Afrifluencers, Africans can inspire and transform minds, boost travel and tourism, and showcase African culture and talent to the world. This paradigm shift in media and entertainment is an opportunity for Africans to take control of their narrative and shape the future of the continent.

Content creation and consumption have undergone a global transformation, with social media platforms like YouTube, TikTok, and Instagram offering unprecedented opportunities for Africans to share their stories and build brands. By leveraging these platforms, Africans can not only generate income but also challenge the one-dimensional narrative perpetuated by Western media. Social media has empowered Africans to tell their own stories and change perceptions both locally and globally.

The rise of social media platforms has allowed Africans to form communities and collaborate on a scale never before possible. By leveraging the power of social media, Africans can go far together and amplify their impact. Platforms like YouTube offer a unique opportunity for Africans to not only share their stories but also build businesses and change lives. By treating social media as a business and adopting a service-oriented mindset, Africans can build thriving communities and drive positive change on the continent.

In this guide, we will outline the blueprint for social media success from an entrepreneurial standpoint. We will cover essential topics such as skill and purpose, success goals, service and value, ambition and discipline, business mindset, technical tasks, content creation, scaling secrets, and diversifying creative capital. By mastering these pillars, Africans can achieve success on social media and contribute to the transformation of the continent. Together, we can bring Africa to the world and shift the narrative for future generations. This is our moment as African content creators to shape the future of Africa with the power of Afrifluence.

INTRODUCTION

B efore embarking on this journey, it is imperative to establish a clear understanding of the terms 'African influencers,' 'Afrifluencers,' and 'Afrifluence.' These terms are not employed casually; rather, they bear significant weight in our discourse. Unlike many African "content creators" who have diluted these terms through overuse, we approach them with sincerity and purpose. Regrettably, certain YouTubers from the continent have tarnished the word's significance by exploiting it for various purposes. Mere participation in online platforms does not warrant the title of influencer. To us, being an influencer entails possessing genuine passion and expertise in a specific domain, thereby adding substantial value—a title earned through diligent effort and exemplary workmanship. Hence, the term 'influence' denotes more than mere presence; it signifies authority and impact, garnered through dedication and excellence in one's craft.

We currently inhabit a digital epoch characterized by fleeting attention spans and an abundance of content choices for consumers. Consequently, advertising paradigms are evolving rapidly, with advertisements morphing into sought-after content. In this guide, our aim is to kindle your enthusiasm for establishing a media enterprise through social media platforms. Our intent is to distill the insights and methodologies cultivated over the past decade to empower you in becoming a brand and a business entity adept at crafting content resonant with contemporary African and African diaspora audiences.

The realm of online video offers opportunities unattainable through traditional television mediums. Social media platforms cater to a profoundly engaged and interconnected demographic, predominantly comprising the younger generation. This demographic craves interactive communication facilitated by both long and short-form content, as well as live interaction—a golden opportunity for aspiring content creators. Unlike television, social media pervades every facet of life, accessible through hundreds of millions of mobile devices globally. By assimilating the knowledge imparted in this guide, you will acquire comprehensive proficiency in delineating and executing a successful content strategy across various social media platforms.

Prior to embarking on your social media odyssey, several fundamental prerequisites warrant attention. It is imperative to establish pertinent digital platforms such as a YouTube channel and other social media pages commensurate with your unique talents and attributes. Procuring a Gmail account aligned with your brand's ethos is paramount.

Subsequently, creating a YouTube channel using this Gmail account serves as a foundational step. Following this preliminary measure, establishing presence on other relevant social media platforms becomes imperative. Mastery of these platforms not only expands your brand's reach but also augments comprehension of the content creation process, thus optimizing long-term results. When christening your social media presence, treat your brand name as the cornerstone of your enterprise, encapsulating your mission and vision.

Collaborating harmoniously with your logo, the brand name embodies the visual identity and ethos of your brand. Whether opting for a direct nomenclature such as

INTRODUCTION

"African Traveller" or adopting a blend of words like "Afritude" or "Afroballer," meticulous consideration should be accorded to crafting a name that resonates with potential followers, leaving a lasting impression indicative of your brand's essence.

Crafting an impactful social media brand name demands meticulous consideration of various factors to ensure seamless communication of your brand's identity, resonance with your target audience, and memorability. Reflection of your brand's identity, ease of recall, relevance to your industry, originality, scalability, availability across platforms, consistency in brand voice, and legal compliance constitute paramount considerations in this endeavor.

Moreover, cognizance of global and continental audiences, alongside strategic utilization of metaphorical naming, acronyms, blending techniques, foreign language integration, location-based nomenclature, linguistic devices, and narrative storytelling can enhance the efficacy and allure of your brand name. Embracing these techniques judiciously and conscientiously will underpin the efficacy of your chosen brand name in reflecting your brand's ethos and resonating with your target demographic.

With the foundational elements in place, the onus shifts to cultivating an audience, establishing authority, delivering value, and monetizing your efforts. Those who have already laid the groundwork can utilize this section as a checklist or bypass it altogether. As promised, our guide traverses from point A to Z in the realm of social media, furnishing you with the knowledge and tools to evolve into a media entity and influencer, thus realizing your African Dream.

Our overarching objective is to empower you to recalibrate the narrative surrounding Africa globally by fostering a legion of media enterprises that control the African brand and narrative, thereby catalyzing economic empowerment and positioning the continent as a digital powerhouse. Early adopters stand to reap the rewards of their foresight and dedication, establishing themselves as authorities within their respective domains not solely by virtue of precedence but, more crucially, through the delivery of unparalleled quality—an attribute we emphasize unequivocally. For further assistance in crafting your brand's narrative, feel free to reach out to us directly at info@panafricanlifestyle.com. Now, let us proceed forth on this transformative journey.

CHAPTER ONE

SKILL AND PURPOSE

Hone your expertise with unwavering dedication. Utilize your distinct skills to soar above all others. Uncover your fundamental purpose and allow your 'why' to be the driving force behind your storytelling endeavors and entrepreneurial pursuits.

In the vibrant world of influencer culture, there exists a profound truth: mastery of skill and a deep understanding of purpose are the twin pillars upon which enduring success is built. To ascend the ranks as a formidable influencer, one must not only refine their craft but also unravel the essence of their passion or talent. True influence, after all, emanates from an authentic connection and purpose-driven content creation.

The journey begins with the discovery of your passion—a fervent love affair with a particular subject or pursuit. Whether it be the culinary arts, the rhythmic dance floor, the art of humor, or the world of haute couture, your passion ignites the flames of creativity and propels you forward in your quest for influence. It is this unwavering devotion to your chosen domain that sustains you through the inevitable trials and tribulations encountered along the way.

Yet, passion alone is not sufficient. It must be coupled with a keen awareness of your innate abilities—the unique gifts bestowed upon you by a higher power. These talents, often overlooked or underappreciated, possess the power to elevate your content and set you apart in a crowded digital landscape. Whether you possess a knack for strategic business planning, a flair for numbers and analytics, or an uncanny eye for captivating visuals, integrating these skills into your brand's DNA adds depth and dimension to your content, resonating with audiences on a deeper level.

At the heart of it all lies purpose—a driving force that transcends mere financial gain and propels you toward a higher calling. Your purpose is your guiding light, illuminating the path ahead and infusing every aspect of your content with meaning and significance. It is the why behind what you do—the raison d'être that propels you forward even in the face of adversity.

AfriFLUENCE

Our own journey with Pan African Lifestyle serves as a testament to the transformative power of passion and purpose. In the nascent stages of our endeavor, we faced numerous challenges, with minimal traction on our social media platforms and scant revenue to show for our efforts. Yet, through unwavering determination and an unshakable belief in our purpose, we persevered, eventually experiencing breakthroughs that propelled our brand to unprecedented heights.

For aspiring influencers, the road to success is paved with dedication, resilience, and an unyielding commitment to one's craft and purpose. By aligning your passion with your talents and imbuing your content with purpose and authenticity, you forge a connection with your audience that transcends the digital realm.

In conclusion, mastery of skill and clarity of purpose are the cornerstones of influencer success. By harnessing the power of passion, leveraging your innate talents, and remaining steadfast in your purpose, you unlock the door to lasting impact and influence in the ever-evolving landscape of social media.

Now that we have a foundational understanding of the principles necessary for building a thriving brand or media company, it's essential to delve deeper into the key components that underpin success: skill, passion, and purpose. Define your skill. Skill is the bedrock upon which excellence is built. It's the learned ability to act with determined results and good execution, often within a given amount of time, energy, or both, in a particular subject or task. Skills can be categorized into two broad types: domain-general and domain-specific. Domain-general skills are versatile and applicable across various fields. These include critical thinking, communication, execution, and attention to detail. As a brand or media company owner, mastering these skills is imperative for success. Creative thinking, effective communication within your medium, and meticulous attention to detail in content creation are essential.

On the other hand, domain-specific skills are unique talents or gifts inherent to individuals. These could range from baking, musical prowess, storytelling, humor, to athletic abilities, among others. These innate skills shape the foundation of your brand and contribute to its uniqueness. While some skills are naturally ingrained in individuals, others require deliberate practice and honing.

However, regardless of origin, mastering the fundamental skills essential for brand building is non-negotiable. While it's impossible to master every skill, understanding the basics and knowing when to outsource or delegate tasks is crucial.

Understand your passion. Passion fuels dedication and perseverance. It's an intense, barely controllable emotion or inclination towards a particular pursuit. True passion is evidenced by an unrelenting obsession with a subject or activity, irrespective of external rewards. As a brand or media company owner, your passion serves as the driving force behind your endeavors. It's what compels you to invest countless hours honing your craft, pushing boundaries, and exploring new horizons. Whether it's African politics, travel and tourism, music, fashion, or any other niche, your passion must run deep.

The concept of the "10,000-hour rule," popularized suggests that expertise is achieved through approximately 10,000 hours of deliberate practice. True passion is evident when individuals willingly invest such extensive time and effort into their chosen pursuit, purely for the joy it brings. Embrace your purpose. Purpose provides direction and meaning to your endeavors. It's the underlying reason for which something is done or created, or for which something exists. A profound sense of purpose gives your actions significance and drives you, especially during challenging times.

Your purpose as a brand or media company owner goes beyond mere profitability or fame. It transcends personal ambitions and encompasses broader societal or altruistic goals. It could be as noble as uplifting local communities, shedding light on underrepresented voices, or championing social causes. Identifying and embracing your purpose is crucial for long-term sustainability and fulfillment. It serves as a guiding light, steering your decisions and actions towards meaningful outcomes. When faced with obstacles or setbacks, reconnecting with your purpose reignites your motivation and determination to persevere. Master and balance the interplay of skill, passion, and purpose. Skill, passion, and purpose are not isolated concepts but interconnected elements that collectively drive success. A mastery of essential skills lays the foundation for excellence, while passion fuels dedication and perseverance. Purpose provides a deeper meaning and direction to your endeavors, guiding you towards impactful outcomes.

As a brand or media company owner, understanding the interplay of these elements is paramount. It's not merely about possessing technical skills or pursuing fleeting interests but aligning your abilities and passions with a greater purpose. This alignment not only fosters personal fulfillment but also enables you to create authentic, resonant content that resonates with your audience. In conclusion, skill, passion, and purpose are the cornerstones upon which successful brands and media companies are built. By cultivating these attributes and leveraging them synergistically, you pave the way for enduring impact and significance in your chosen field.

This entire chapter underscores a profound message encapsulated in a simple yet powerful phrase: "Take your craft seriously and pursue it with love, dedication, and unwavering commitment." As an African influencer, your role transcends mere representation of your personal brand; rather, you are entrusted with the responsibility of serving as a beacon for the continent. In the eyes of the world, Afrifluencers embody the spirit and essence of Africa, acting as ambassadors who carry the aspirations, culture, and values of an entire continent.

It is imperative to recognize that every action you take, every word you speak, and every project you undertake carries immense weight, not only for yourself but also for your country and the broader African community. Your dedication to honing your skills and mastering your domain not only enhances your personal credibility but also elevates the reputation of your country and contributes to changing the narrative surrounding Africa.

Furthermore, infusing your work with love is paramount. Love is the driving force behind authenticity and genuine connection. When you approach your craft with love, you infuse it with a unique energy and passion that resonates with your audience on a deeper level. This authenticity attracts like-minded individuals who share your values and vision, fostering a sense of community and belonging.

By cultivating a deep connection with your audience, you have the power to influence minds and shape behaviors, particularly in shaping perceptions of Africa. Through your work, you have the opportunity to challenge stereotypes, dismantle misconceptions, and showcase the rich diversity and untapped potential of the continent.

In essence, by taking your craft seriously and infusing it with love, you not only elevate yourself but also uplift your country and Africa as a whole. You become a catalyst for positive change, inspiring others to embrace their passions, pursue excellence, and contribute to the collective growth and prosperity of Africa.

CHAPTER TWO

SUCCESS GOAL

Your success transcends mere financial gain. It embodies the achievement and ongoing pursuit of a holistic purpose that encompasses every aspect of your life. This purpose encompasses your spiritual, physical, mental, personal, and financial ambitions.

Individuals who achieve success in life invariably possess clearly defined goals for success. Though these goals may vary significantly from person to person, the fundamental characteristic shared by every successful individual is their prior identification of what they aspire to achieve. As one progresses through life and gains exposure to new experiences, it's natural for these goals to evolve. However, having a defined target is essential for achieving a level of universal success.

For instance, a significant goal for social media accounts should be to acquire 1,000 true fans or community members—individuals who are part of your tribe and follow your brand's journey with unwavering support and emotional connection. Building an audience of 1,000 true tribe members lays the foundation for establishing a robust online community and an offline following.

This principle holds true for those aspiring to become content creators and, ultimately, owners of media companies. Aspiring to become a successful influencer requires establishing life goals, which serve as guiding lights illuminating the path toward one's desired destination. From a financial perspective, envisioning a particular lifestyle or level of comfort necessitates understanding the resources required to attain such aspirations. Similarly, aspiring to achieve physical fitness requires identifying the necessary training regimen to sculpt one's ideal physique. In the realm of social media success, introspection is crucial. Individuals must candidly assess their desired domain of mastery and aspire to be acknowledged as authority figures within specific niches.

Clarifying these objectives is paramount for devising a concrete action plan geared towards achievement. Some individuals prefer to document their goals in a journal, while others opt for a vision board. Regardless of the method chosen, the key is to encapsulate these aspirations in tangible form. Reflecting on the inception of Pan African Lifestyle, it became evident that envisioning the brand as both a lifestyle entity and a media company, with aspirations of achieving a six-figure revenue and establishing a robust brand presence globally, laid the foundation for subsequent success. Recognizing that the business model would encompass more than just advertising and sponsorship but also services was pivotal.

The journey of Wode Maya exemplifies the power of setting incremental goals aligned with one's passion and purpose. From initially seeking capital to travel African countries and showcase a positive narrative of the continent to subsequently expanding his vision to bridge Africa with the world, his trajectory underscores the importance of setting tangible objectives. Maya's evolution from short-term goals to long-term aspirations of impacting the economy of Africa through media entrepreneurship demonstrates the transformative potential of incremental goal-setting.

Indeed, each accomplished goal serves as a stepping stone toward the realization of larger aspirations. Thousands of hours of dedication culminated in the attainment of significant milestones, such as reaching one million subscribers on YouTube. This journey underscores the gradual and progressive nature of success goals, wherein each achievement propels one toward the next target. The concept of "1,000 true fans" played a major factor in the success of Wode Maya and other influencers. Many content creators don't necessarily need millions of fans or customers. Instead, they just need a dedicated base of "true fans" who are passionate about their work.

These are fans who will buy anything they produce, whether it's a product, service, or piece of art because they know they add value, trust them, and are invested in the journey and experience. They're the ones who will attend their shows, purchase their merchandise, and support them through thick and thin. The number 1,000 is somewhat arbitrary—it could be more or less depending on the situation—but the point is that mass appeal isn't necessary to sustain financially. With just 1,000 true fans who are willing to spend an average of $100 per year on their work, they could potentially generate $100,000 in revenue annually.

The concept highlights the importance of having the goal of building a deep, meaningful connection with the audience rather than chasing superficial popularity. By focusing on cultivating a devoted following, they can create a sustainable career doing what they love.

In the realm of influencer marketing, selecting the appropriate category of influencer is paramount for brands seeking authentic engagement. Mega-influencers, with their expansive reach, are compelling for brands aiming for broad exposure, albeit at a higher cost. Macro-influencers offer a balance of reach and engagement, leveraging their reputation to command attention. Mid-tier influencers, although lacking celebrity status, possess a dedicated following and offer a blend of reach and authenticity. Micro-influencers, with their niche focus and intimate connection with followers, often yield high engagement rates and foster trust among their audience.

For personal and corporate brands operating within the advertising and sponsorship model, defining goals that encompass the business model and value proposition is essential. Whether offering courses, consulting, or social media management services, delineating creative and business objectives is imperative. Additionally, considering the nature of the media company—whether it focuses on original programming, content aggregation, or personality-driven branding—further refines the goal-setting process.

Ultimately, success in the realm of social media hinges on a strategic alignment of goals with audience interests across diverse platforms. By setting clear objectives and navigating the journey with purpose and determination, individuals can chart a course toward enduring success as influencers and media entrepreneurs.

CHAPTER THREE

SERVICE AND VALUE

By dedicating yourself to serving others and evolving your craft into a system that addresses public demands, you elevate both yourself and your enterprise to the status of a necessity. Through proactive endeavors, your outcomes are esteemed highly, and as individuals recognize the utility of your services, your intrinsic value escalates—this is the quintessence of value addition.

To achieve success in any endeavor, including navigating the complex landscape of social media, it is imperative to discern how your offerings cater to the needs of your audience. Whether you provide laughter, motivation, style guidance, or financial education, each serves a purpose. It is essential for any brand to swiftly identify the unique need it satisfies. Understanding both the nature of your offerings and their value enables you to refine and enhance your delivery.

Audiences value the certainty of finding content that reliably delivers a specific experience. Be it education, entertainment, fitness, lifestyle improvement, or personal grooming tips, your content fulfills a crucial need. The global landscape teems with potential viewers seeking exactly what you propose to create or are in the process of building. Adopting a service-oriented mindset and consistently delivering your content will naturally attract the right audience.

Take, for example, Wode Maya's channel mission to alter the perception of Africa. Through a blend of educational and entertaining content, he aims to present Africa in a light that instills pride in both continental Africans and the diaspora. This mission encapsulates the essence of the service he provides.

Moreover, individuals like Wode Maya not only produce engaging and transformative content but also engage in philanthropy, further enriching their audience's experience. Such efforts, alongside those of others like Ashley Cleveland and the Ashley in Afrika brand, have cultivated a deep sense of trust and loyalty among viewers, providing them with valuable insights into African life, travel, and investment opportunities. The emotional bond forged through this content has even inspired members of the diaspora to relocate to Africa, a testament to the profound impact of our work.

It is crucial to recognize that the value offered through your media company extends beyond tangible rewards. Value can manifest as a positive emotion, such as the joy or stress relief your viewers experience, or in practical benefits, such as financial gains or improved health from adhering to your advice. YouTube, at its core, is a platform for service, offering videos as the product and the transformative effect on viewers' lives as the ultimate value. By focusing on serving others and honing your ability to transform your channel into a vibrant media company, you pave the way for enduring success.

In the dynamic realm of media and branding, the interplay between "Service" and "Value" takes on a nuanced and pivotal role, particularly when our focus shifts towards our audience. "Service," within this context, encapsulates the delivery of content and experiences that resonate, educate, or entertain, functioning without the exchange of physical commodities. It's about crafting and delivering content that stands out for its expertise, convenience, timeliness, and innovative insight. This could range from exclusive interviews and investigative journalism to engaging entertainment and cutting-edge digital storytelling.

On the flip side, "Value" transcends mere economic metrics, embodying the relevance, impact, and significance our content and brand experiences hold for our audience. It's inherently subjective, shaped by individual preferences, cultural trends, and the unique manner in which our audience interacts with our content. Beyond economics, value embodies the principles and ethics we stand for, weaving them into the fabric of our brand identity.

Central to this discourse is "Perceived Value," a concept that captures the essence of what our audience believes our content and brand experiences are worth. It's a multifaceted perception, influenced not just by the content's intrinsic attributes but also by our brand's reputation, the quality of interaction we offer, and the emotional journeys we facilitate. Perceived value is the linchpin in understanding the audience's engagement, loyalty, and willingness to embrace our brand.

Several dimensions shape perceived value in the media landscape. Functional value is the practical utility our content offers, whether it solves a problem, provides key information, or fulfills a specific need for our audience. Emotional value is the ability of our content and brand to evoke feelings, from the joy of discovery to the thrill of being part of a community or movement. Social Value refers to how our content enhances the audience's social standing or identity, acting as a badge of cultural currency or intellectual capital.

Monetary Value: The cost versus benefit analysis our audience conducts, assessing whether the content or experience is worth their time, attention, or subscription. Convenience value is the ease and accessibility of engaging with our content, ensuring that we meet our audience where they are, in ways that seamlessly fit into their lives.

In the competitive arena of media and branding, amplifying perceived value is not just a strategy but a necessity. It involves elevating our content quality, leveraging influential collaborations, sparking meaningful conversations, and continuously innovating to exceed audience expectations. Every piece of content, every interaction, every story we tell should be a stepping stone towards reinforcing our brand image and deepening our audience connection. Understanding the symbiosis between service and value is crucial for media entities aiming to make an indelible mark. Our service—be it through captivating narratives, insightful analysis, or groundbreaking visuals—must embody the value we promise to deliver. It's about aligning our offerings with the audience's evolving needs and aspirations, thereby not just meeting but exceeding their expectations.

For you, as a media influencer or content creator, recognizing and nurturing this relationship between service and value becomes your compass. It guides your content strategy, shapes your brand narrative, and ultimately, measures the impact you have on your audience. This understanding not only directs the content you produce but also ensures it resonates, engages, and adds meaningful value to the cultural tapestry of your audience's lives.

It is imperative for us to underscore that, in our perspective, offering service and value transcends merely replicating existing models. The notion that every individual must embody the archetype of an African travel vlogger, embarked on a mission to alter the continent's narrative by revealing aspects seldom covered by mainstream media, or endeavoring to visit all 54 countries, is not a requisite for everyone. While we in no way denigrate these particular focal points, it is crucial to recognize that those imbued with a genuine zeal for exploring Africa, coupled with a unique ability to present the continent in a novel light, are poised for success. African vloggers who distinguish themselves through their singular personalities, compelling narratives, and engaging content are likely to thrive. Our observation is that this path has become somewhat saturated, not necessarily pursued out of a genuine desire but perhaps because it mirrors the trajectory of others who have found success in this niche.

Furthermore, it is not incumbent upon every member of the African diaspora to return to the continent with the intention of inaugurating a travel or consulting firm. This statement is not meant to belittle such endeavors but to illuminate the myriad opportunities that exist beyond this scope. It is also to acknowledge those professionals within the outlined domains who are excelling and delivering exceptional value, including but not limited to luminaries like Ashley in Afrika, Wode Maya, Tayo Aina, Steven Ndwuku, Vanessa Kanbi, the Odana Network, African Tigress, among others.

In addition, individuals are making significant impacts in areas such as comedy, with notable figures like Josh2Funny and SamSpedy; in Afrodance, with talents such as Dancegod Lloyd and Afronitaaa; and in fitness, with influencers like Brian Syuki and Afrifitness leading the charge. The purpose of enumerating these diverse Afrifluencers is to highlight the breadth of opportunities available across various niches. The realm of gaming, tech reviews, fashion commentary, and culinary arts also offers ample space for growth and innovation. Embracing the role of an African influencer need not be confined to the portrayal of the continent's countries, luxury real estate, or the lifestyles of the affluent—unless such themes genuinely resonate with one's passion.

CHAPTER FOUR

AMBITION AND DISCIPLINE

A profound and unwavering desire to achieve greatness serves as the cornerstone for reaching the highest peaks of success. This fervent aspiration provides the fuel and motivation needed to overcome obstacles and persevere through challenges along the journey. However, it is not merely enough to possess this burning desire; one must also exhibit disciplined behavior and adhere rigorously to a well-constructed plan. Consistently staying committed to the strategic roadmap laid out ensures that each step taken is purposeful and aligned with the overarching goal. This steadfast dedication to the plan fosters resilience in the face of adversity and empowers individuals to navigate through the complexities of their endeavors with unwavering resolve. Thus, while ambition may provide the initial spark, it is the consistent practice of adhering to the plan that ultimately propels individuals towards the pinnacle of success.

The allure of the social media lifestyle may appear glamorous and enticing, but it's crucial not to be swayed by surface appearances. Behind the glitz lies an immense amount of hard work and dedication. It's a misconception that success on social media comes effortlessly; in reality, it demands relentless effort and commitment. Each post created requires meticulous attention to detail and a consistent level of quality to captivate audiences and garner attention. Maintaining consistency is paramount in the realm of content creation. Without a steadfast commitment to delivering excellence with every post, one's content risks being overlooked amidst the vast sea of posts available. Simply put, without consistency, both your content and your profile are at risk of fading into obscurity.

While ambition serves as a powerful driving force, it must be accompanied by discipline to yield meaningful results. Ambition ignites passion and provides purpose, fueling your aspirations and inspiring you to dream big. Yet, it's discipline that transforms those dreams into reality through consistent action. Many aspiring social media influencers falter due to a lack of discipline. They struggle to improve their content or maintain a regular posting schedule, leading to stagnation and frustration. Despite the challenges, successful influencers persevere by steadily advancing, one step at a time. This perseverance is fueled by discipline, ensuring that progress continues even when results seem elusive.

Ambition and discipline play crucial roles in navigating the landscape of social media. Ambition fuels the desire to excel, setting lofty goals and envisioning success. It's the driving force behind your aspirations to grow your audience, increase engagement, and establish yourself as an influential figure in your niche. Discipline, on the other hand, is what turns those aspirations into tangible achievements. It's the commitment to consistent action and the willingness to put in the necessary work day in and day out. In the context of social media, discipline manifests in several ways: Posting frequency is key.

Consistently posting high-quality content is essential for maintaining relevance and visibility on social media platforms. Setting a goal to post 4-5 times per day requires discipline to create and curate content regularly, ensuring that your audience remains engaged and your profile stays active. Execution of objectives is important. Personal objectives, such as going live on social media platforms, require discipline to follow through. It's not enough to simply have the ambition to engage with your audience in real-time; you must also commit to scheduling and executing these live sessions according to plan. Engagement and analysis are crucial to proper execution. Discipline involves dedicating time to actively engage with your community and analyze the performance of your content. This includes responding to comments, messages, and mentions, as well as studying analytics to understand what resonates with your audience and what the algorithm recommends in your niche.

By combining ambition with discipline, social media users can effectively leverage these platforms to achieve their goals. Whether it's growing a following, increasing engagement, or building a brand, the synergy between ambition and discipline is key to success in the dynamic world of social media. In essence, ambition without discipline is futile. It's the combination of passion and perseverance, guided by a strong work ethic, that paves the way for success in the competitive landscape of social media. So, while it's crucial to dream big and aspire to greatness, it's equally important to cultivate the discipline necessary to turn those aspirations into achievements, post by post, day by day. Having ambition as an Afrifluencer entails having a vision large enough to identify a blueprint from influencers who have achieved remarkable success at a major scale – the pinnacle of achievement within the industry. It involves envisioning the trajectory of one's brand to emulate and even surpass those accomplishments. This ambitious vision serves as a guiding beacon, inspiring the Afrifluencer to reverse engineer the path to success, starting from the beginning.

However, ambition alone is not enough. It must be complemented by discipline – the discipline to conduct thorough research, analyze trends, and understand the strategies that have propelled influencers to great heights. It requires a commitment to taking deliberate steps, even if it means iterating, refining, and re-posting content to align with the desired trajectory. Discipline empowers the Afrifluencer to stay focused on their goals, navigate challenges, and persistently pursue excellence, ensuring that every action taken contributes to the realization of their ambitious vision.

CHAPTER FIVE

BUSINESS MINDSET

The next level involves transitioning from mere skill or passion into a sustainable enterprise, where your craft becomes the foundation of a thriving business. It requires cultivating a mindset that sees your abilities not just as a hobby or talent but as a valuable commodity capable of generating income. This transformation entails establishing an entrepreneurial attitude that drives you to monetize your skills effectively, turning your passion into a profitable venture.

Business Business leaders wield significant global influence, a widely acknowledged fact stemming from their distinct mindset—a knack for perceiving opportunities in every sphere. Entrepreneurs possess this transformative mindset, turning encounters into lucrative ventures. If you aim for success in your social media endeavors, adopting this entrepreneurial mindset is paramount. To command respect in social media, take it seriously yourself. This doesn't entail rushing to copyright or trademark your channel name, nor mastering the system instantaneously. Such transitions require time. However, aligning your approach with business principles will fundamentally alter your decision-making processes.

Instead of treating your social media presence as a mere pastime or a platform for sporadic attempts at virality, envision it as a media enterprise. Every piece of content you publish becomes a proprietary product of your social media domain. Your audience becomes your clientele, while algorithms and statistics serve as your content ledger. Access to detailed viewership and engagement metrics grants you insights comparable to those of major conglomerates. Understanding that social media operates as a business is crucial; embracing this realization early on will set you on a path to prosperity.

While this entrepreneurial mindset may not have been inherent from the outset, its adoption became imperative as our platforms flourished. We now regard our social media realms as integral facets of a larger media conglomerate. Consequently, I've assembled a dedicated team to advance our yearly objectives. Embracing this perspective has enabled us to recognize our worth as content creators and media proprietors. Moreover, it has facilitated the pursuit of sponsorship and partnership opportunities from a position of business acumen rather than mere influence. Recognizing oneself as a business owner fundamentally alters one's approach, prioritizing audience value delivery to maximize market influence.

Our evolution into the most influential Pan African brand and a diaspora information hub has rendered us attractive to corporate collaborators. This standing has been bestowed upon us by our PAL (Pan African Lifestyle) audience. By offering value through our content and fostering audience engagement, we've augmented our standing as a media entity. This, in turn, empowers us to negotiate with multinational corporations, leveraging our distinct audience and meeting specific market demands.

How can you similarly metamorphose your media venture into a sustainable business? Identify the niche you serve within the social media landscape. Assess your audience's engagement and loyalty. Is your social media presence a recognizable brand or merely a nondescript account? Transforming your mindset from content creator to business proprietor will elevate your influence and viability in the digital marketplace.

Many African influencers embark on their social media journey with the primary goal of harnessing their brand's potential within an advertising-centric business model. While advertising undoubtedly presents a lucrative avenue for income generation, it's imperative for media brands to broaden their horizons beyond mere sponsorship, particularly in the African landscape.

Diversification is key to long-term sustainability and growth in the media industry. One often overlooked alternative to the traditional advertising model is the service business model. This approach involves leveraging the influencer's brand and media presence to offer specialized services, thereby unlocking additional revenue streams and profit opportunities.

By diversifying their revenue streams through the service business model, influencers can mitigate the inherent risks associated with relying solely on advertising revenue. Moreover, this approach fosters deeper connections with their audience by providing value-added services that extend beyond traditional content consumption.

Furthermore, embracing the service business model empowers African influencers to contribute meaningfully to their local economies. By offering services such as content creation, digital marketing, or social media management, they not only generate income for themselves but also create employment opportunities within their communities, thereby fostering economic growth and empowerment.

In conclusion, while advertising remains a prominent revenue stream for African influencers, embracing the service business model opens up a world of opportunities for sustainable growth and diversification. By leveraging their brand and expertise to offer specialized services, influencers can not only enhance their financial resilience but also make a positive impact on their communities and industries at large.

Afrifluencers often navigate their digital journey through two primary business models: the Advertising Model and the Service Model. The Advertising Model serves as the cornerstone for many content creators, where revenue is primarily generated through sponsored content, brand partnerships, and advertisements displayed on their platforms. This model places a significant emphasis on building a large audience base to attract advertisers, often prioritizing quantity of content over depth or specialization. Growth within this model is driven by increasing audience reach and engagement to attract more advertisers and higher-paying partnerships.

On the other hand, the Service Model offers an alternative approach for Afrifluencers to monetize their expertise and niche. Instead of relying solely on advertising revenue, content creators leverage their skills to offer specialized services such as consulting, content creation, or training. This model focuses on providing value-added services that cater to specific needs or problems within their target audience or industry. Revenue is directly tied to the delivery of services, often through one-time fees, retainer agreements, or subscription models. Scalability within the Service Model is achieved by expanding service offerings, acquiring new clients, and establishing expertise within their field, allowing for more diversified income streams.

Afrifluencers can strategically leverage both models to scale their media company business and social media brand. By cultivating partnerships with brands and optimizing their platforms for advertising revenue, they can capitalize on the benefits of the Advertising Model. Simultaneously, by identifying their unique skills and offering tailored services such as consulting or content creation, they can tap into the opportunities presented by the Service Model. Combining both models allows Afrifluencers to diversify their revenue streams, reducing dependency on any single source of income. Moreover, the synergy between the two models enables them to deepen engagement with their audience, attract higher-paying advertising partnerships, and provide greater value to both their clients and followers.

Having a business mindset as an Afrifluencer involves more than just creating content; it's about viewing yourself as a media company and structuring deals accordingly. This means approaching partnerships and collaborations with the mindset of a business, negotiating terms that align with your brand values and revenue goals. By adopting this perspective, Afrifluencers can elevate themselves beyond mere content creators to become strategic partners for brands, offering unique value propositions and driving mutually beneficial outcomes.

When operating as a media company, Afrifluencers have the opportunity to structure deals in a way that maximizes their revenue potential and establishes long-term partnerships. This may involve diversifying income streams beyond traditional advertising by offering specialized services, such as sponsored content packages, brand consulting, or social media management. By developing a comprehensive system that outlines their offerings, pricing strategies, and terms of engagement, Afrifluencers can streamline the negotiation process and position themselves as professional partners in the industry.

Moreover, embracing a business-to-business (B2B) approach allows Afrifluencers to transcend the limitations of a strictly business-to-customer (B2C) model. By viewing themselves as entities that cater to both brands and their audience, Afrifluencers can unlock new opportunities for collaboration and revenue generation. This shift in perspective enables Afrifluencers to negotiate deals that not only benefit their personal brand but also contribute to the growth and success of the businesses they partner with.

While there's nothing inherently wrong with focusing solely on the advertising model and negotiating deals based on personality, it can be limiting in terms of long-term sustainability and growth. By embracing a business mindset and structuring deals as a media company, Afrifluencers can expand their revenue streams, deepen their impact, and establish themselves as key players in the digital media landscape. Ultimately, it's about recognizing the value you bring to the table and leveraging that value to forge strategic partnerships that drive success for all parties involved.

CHAPTER SIX

TECHNICAL TASKS

Mastering the technical aspects of any craft often garners little excitement among the masses. Yet, those who do attain proficiency in these technical nuances gain a notable advantage. Practical experience transforms one into a practitioner, delving into the intricate science behind their craft, ultimately becoming the engine that drives income generation.

Technical tasks are often overlooked in social media success, with many perceiving content creation on platforms like YouTube as merely recording and uploading videos. However, the reality is far more intricate. Simply knowing how to upload a video does not guarantee success; becoming proficient in technical aspects is key. To succeed, one must become a practitioner, understanding foundational elements such as video creation, editing, crafting appealing thumbnails, and creating catchy titles. By mastering these fundamentals, individuals position themselves for success in the competitive landscape of social media.

Before diving into quality content creation, there are essential prerequisites. Establishing a social media channel involves configuring default settings, reaching specific subscriber and watch hour thresholds, and becoming eligible for the Social Media Partner Program. Once these foundational steps are completed, individuals are equipped with the basic framework to commence their social media journey as a business entity.

Success often stems from observing and learning from established channels within one's niche, gaining valuable insights into content creation. This doesn't necessitate mastering complex software but rather finding a process that works and consistently applying oneself to cultivate channel growth.

In the realm of social media, mastering technical tasks such as editing, copywriting, crafting engaging captions, selecting compelling thumbnails, choosing the right audio piece, ensuring visual appeal, and maintaining a cohesive design theme are crucial across all platforms. Effective editing enhances the overall quality of content, ensuring it flows smoothly and captivates the audience's attention. Similarly, copywriting skills play a vital role in crafting engaging titles and descriptions that entice viewers to click and engage further. Additionally, selecting visually appealing thumbnails is essential for attracting clicks and increasing video views.

Furthermore, selecting the appropriate audio piece to accompany content can significantly impact its overall appeal and engagement. Whether it's background music to set the tone or sound effects to enhance storytelling, audio plays a crucial role in enhancing the viewer's experience. Moreover, paying attention to visual appeal and maintaining a consistent design theme helps establish brand identity and fosters recognition among the audience.

Optimizing the channel for content discovery is essential for exponential growth. High-quality content coupled with well-executed technical tasks creates a system that generates passive income. Attention to detail, such as optimizing metadata, creating captivating thumbnails, and incorporating annotations, elevates the professionalism of the channel, fostering trust and loyalty among viewers.

A successful social media channel encompasses editorial, social media, and marketing components. Utilizing metrics and data analysis to tailor content to the audience's preferences is crucial for sustained success. YouTube, for instance, prioritizes watch time as a metric of success, reflecting the platform's goal of maximizing ad revenue through viewer engagement.

Measuring success on social media involves assessing metrics such as subscriber conversion, viewer retention, and audience engagement. By executing technical tasks meticulously and analyzing data effectively, individuals can refine their strategies and improve their social media systems, ultimately driving growth and success in the dynamic digital landscape.

Technical tasks and skills in social media and content creation encompass a wide range of activities contributing to the creation, optimization, and distribution of digital content. Starting with video editing, proficiency in software such as Adobe Premiere Pro, Final Cut Pro, or DaVinci Resolve is crucial for refining and enhancing video content. Beginners can explore free versions like iMovie or online tools such as Canva, Kittl, ChatGPT, offering user-friendly interfaces and basic editing capabilities. Graphic design skills are important for creating visually appealing graphics, logos, and branding elements. Beginners can start with free tools like Canva, offering templates and customization options. In addition to graphic design, copywriting plays a significant role in crafting compelling written content for video titles, descriptions, captions, and social media posts.

Creating eye-catching thumbnail images is important for attracting viewers and enticing them to click on content. Tools like Canva or Kittl offer customizable templates for attention-grabbing thumbnails. Knowledge of audio editing software is necessary to enhance sound quality or add background music. Understanding SEO principles is crucial to optimize content for search engines and improve visibility on social media platforms. Content planning and scheduling skills are necessary for creating content calendars and scheduling posts for optimal timing and engagement. Community management skills involve engaging with followers, responding to comments and messages, and fostering a sense of community around the brand or content. Professionals should be adept at understanding platform-specific features and best practices for platforms like YouTube, Instagram, TikTok, Twitter, and Facebook.

Finally, continuous learning and adaptation are key for staying ahead in the ever-evolving landscape of social media and content creation. Professionals should stay updated on industry trends, algorithm changes, and new features on social media platforms, adapting content strategies accordingly. By continually honing their skills and staying informed about the latest developments, content creators can build a successful online presence and thrive in the competitive world of social media.

CHAPTER SEVEN

CONTENT CREATION

Content reigns supreme in the digital realm. The visual, audio, and print expressions of your work are what distinguish you in a sea of creators. It's imperative to master the art of generating quality content that not only simulates experiences but also effectively communicates ideas, stories, perceptions, and emotions. Compelling content has the power to motivate people to share, like, subscribe, and most importantly, watch.

B efore delving into video creation, it's essential to craft a comprehensive content plan aligned with your platform's objectives and resonating with your target audience. Defining a strategically relevant content domain sets the stage for success, positioning you at the intersection of your passion and your audience's interests. Consider what unique value your brand can bring to consumers to earn their loyalty. For instance, sharing captivating stories from the motherland or offering insights into thriving in Africa presents a narrative differing from mainstream perceptions.

Compelling videos serve as a gateway to attract new viewers, introduce them to your content ecosystem, and cultivate a devoted fanbase. While no strict rules govern content creation on social media platforms, fundamental principles have emerged as crucial for crafting a successful strategy. Viewers crave personal connections and authenticity. Thus, conveying why you do what you do, articulating your platform's core values, and demonstrating dedication to serving your audience are vital.

Attention is paramount in content creation. Your ultimate goal is to captivate and retain your audience's interest without resorting to sensationalism or inauthenticity. Prioritize creating content with your end users in mind, and develop a systematic approach to production to maintain consistency and avoid burnout. Initially, this may involve using basic editing applications and progressing to leveraging external resources like building a team or outsourcing projects for quality and consistency.

Every element, from thumbnails to descriptions, shapes your audience's perception of your brand and media company. Take a holistic approach to creativity, considering not just the final product but also the production process. The focus should be on creating quality content that resonates with your audience, fostering engagement and fulfilling promises made to viewers.

A notable shift in content production revolves around adopting a "documenting over creating" mindset, championing authenticity and urging creators to embrace their true selves. This approach involves sharing unfiltered moments from life, capturing genuine experiences, and fostering deeper connections and engagement with the audience.

Documenting, rather than creating, allows creators to showcase the essence of their brand in its most unadulterated form, ultimately fostering a more impactful and genuine online presence. By prioritizing authenticity and transparency, creators can cultivate trust and relatability among viewers, strengthening the bond with their audience.

Content creation encompasses various mediums beyond videos and images, including audio, writing, and articles. Repurposing content across different formats and platforms allows creators to reach a broader audience and establish a stronger online presence. Embracing both virtual and physical avenues of content creation enables creators to diversify their offerings, cater to different audience preferences, and enhance their overall impact and influence.

CHAPTER EIGHT

SCALING SECRETS

Establishing a solid foundation is essential to laying the groundwork for the exponential expansion of your media company. This involves not only envisioning your goals but also devising comprehensive strategies to achieve them. Scaling, in essence, is about more than just growth— it's about systematically implementing processes and systems that will not only facilitate expansion but also ensure sustainability and efficiency.

To embark on the journey of scaling, conducting a thorough assessment of your current operations is imperative. Identify areas of strength and opportunities for improvement by analyzing existing workflows, resources, and technologies. Pinpointing bottlenecks and inefficiencies that may hinder growth is crucial. Once identified, the next step is to develop and implement scalable solutions tailored to your company's unique needs and goals. This may involve streamlining workflows, adopting new technologies, or investing in talent development to enhance productivity and innovation.

Furthermore, scaling requires a forward-thinking approach that anticipates future challenges and opportunities. Stay agile and adaptable in the face of evolving market trends, social media algorithms, user experience changes, and consumer preferences. Foster a culture of innovation and continuous improvement within your organization by encouraging experimentation and learning from both successes and failures. Building strong partnerships and networks within your industry ecosystem is also essential. Collaborating with like-minded companies and influencers can expand your reach and provide valuable insights and reso urces to fuel your growth journey.

Moreover, scaling requires a commitment to ongoing monitoring and evaluation to track progress and adjust strategies as needed. Implement key performance indicators (KPIs) to measure success, regularly review processes and systems, and solicit feedback from stakeholders, including your audiences on each platform. Key performance indicators should go beyond basic metrics, focusing on engagement metrics such as comments, shares, and audience reactions. In essence, scaling your media company requires careful planning, execution, and adaptation. Lay the groundwork for sustainable growth and foster a culture of innovation and collaboration to position your company for long-term success in an ever-changing digital landscape.

At this stage, with a substantial subscriber base, you aim to elevate your brand and social media presence to become an authority in your domain. Understanding social media algorithms and user experience is crucial. Quality content over quantity becomes paramount. You've earned respect; now set yourself apart professionally and financially. Investing in yourself and your business is necessary. Creating content that captivates viewers from start to finish is key. After mastering content quality, diversify income streams beyond advertising revenue.

Successful Afrifluencers incorporate various revenue streams like affiliate marketing, merchandise, publications, or real estate investments. Invest in branding elements like a website, theme song, logo, and sound signature. Consider paid membership options or subscription-based alternatives. Seek sponsorship opportunities aligned with your vision. Implementing these strategies increases revenue and creates automatic income-producing assets. The goal is to build a self-sufficient brand that runs almost on autopilot, allowing you to focus on scaling while trustworthy teammates implement the system.

CHAPTER NINE

DIVERSIFY INVESTMENTS

Transitioning towards an eclectic portfolio of income-producing assets stands as the cornerstone of acquiring generational wealth. It necessitates honing the adeptness to leverage your income across a spectrum of investments, each possessing the potential to appreciate significantly over time. This strategic diversification not only mitigates risk but also fosters long-term financial stability and prosperity, positioning you and your descendants for sustained wealth accumulation and security.

The pinnacle of your Afrifluence journey hinges on transforming your media company into a diverse array of offline income-generating assets. Our commitment extends beyond digital platforms to tangible investments, notably in real estate across Africa. We aim to cultivate real experiences and events where Pan-Africans converge, exchanging ideas, forging connections, and catalyzing action and investment for the continent's advancement.

Our vision entails elevating Pan African Lifestyle from a media company to a comprehensive lifestyle brand. This expansion includes real estate development, business and personal development summits, and exclusive inner-circle experiences. These initiatives not only facilitate physical ownership of assets on the continent but also enable us to make a tangible impact, mirroring our online efforts in the real world.

Recognizing your media company as a tool, a vehicle, and an experience is essential. You can utilize it individually or in combination to streamline your life, amplify your influence, or craft a distinct virtual realm where your audience deeply engages. Our recommendation? Embrace all facets to maximize your potential.

Building on our social media success, we leverage our platform's income to diversify into various economic opportunities within Africa. This includes acquiring companies, media outlets, resorts, mining ventures, and more – all aligned with our vision and brand ethos. Our objective isn't merely to accumulate wealth but to establish robust online and offline enterprises driven by our media company and lifestyle brand.

We encourage every Afrifluencer to capitalize on their digital success by venturing into offline opportunities while continuing to invest in online assets like content. Whether you're a food critic, a fashion influencer, or an automotive expert, expanding into physical ventures such as restaurants, stores, or dealerships complements your online presence and fosters lasting legacies.

The true power of social media lies not just in owning a media company but in time ownership and leverage. By delegating responsibilities to a capable team, you gain the freedom to focus on strategic growth and impact. This signifies the pinnacle of Afrifluence – using your platform to drive entrepreneurship, philanthropy, and lasting change throughout Africa.

In conclusion, as an African influencer, you have transformed your media company into a versatile tool, a powerful vehicle, and an immersive experience. How you wield this influence to shape the future of the continent is entirely up to you.

CHAPTER TEN

CONCLUSION

Being an African influencer transcends mere title; it entails a profound responsibility. With meticulous care, we've distilled a decade of social media expertise, coupled with insights from influential voices across the continent and its diaspora, to craft a roadmap to triumph. Within these pages lies the blueprint for realizing The African Dream and ascending to the pinnacle of Afrifluence.

Begin by delving deep within, uncovering your innate talents, and defining your purpose with clarity and conviction. Envision your success with unwavering clarity, setting ambitious goals that propel you forward. Cement your identity by delineating the invaluable service you offer and the profound value you bestow upon your audience. Root yourself in ambition, embracing discipline as your steadfast ally in the pursuit of greatness.

CONCLUSIONS

Adopt a business-minded approach to your social media endeavors, treating your platform as a thriving enterprise deserving of strategic acumen. Lay a solid foundation through meticulous attention to technical minutiae, ensuring the stability and longevity of your media empire.

Elevate your craft by mastering the art of consistently delivering top-tier content that captivates and resonates with your audience. When excellence becomes your standard, unlock the secrets of scaling, transforming your output into an unparalleled force of influence.

As you ascend to the esteemed status of Afrifluence, transcending mere online success to embody a beacon of inspiration, it becomes imperative to diversify your investments. Venture beyond the digital realm, seizing tangible assets and real-world opportunities that fortify your legacy and extend your impact far beyond cyberspace.

This is the vision that propels our media company forward – rooted in the celebration of Afrocentrism, the propagation of The African Dream, and the cultivation of thriving communities both online and offline. We are driven not solely by financial gain but by a deep-seated commitment to uplift and empower the people of Africa, nurturing a new generation of entrepreneurs and visionaries who will shape the continent's future.

As you harness the immense power of Afrifluence, let your influence reverberate as a force for good across the motherland. Embrace your role as a catalyst for change, a champion of progress, and a custodian of The African Dream. In this noble pursuit lies the true essence of Afrifluence – not just as a means of personal enrichment but as a conduit for collective upliftment and transformation.

AUTHORS

E mmanuel Bope and Solange Bope, the visionary authors behind "Live The African Dream" and "Afrifluence," epitomize the epitome of Pan-African entrepreneurship and empowerment. Drawing from their extensive experience as entrepreneurs and learning from the crucible of trials and errors, they have ascended to establish Pan African Lifestyle (PAL), the preeminent Pan-African media company and lifestyle brand globally.

Renowned as the social media and branding savants of Africa, Emmanuel and Solange have devoted their lives to empowering Africans across the continent and the diaspora, exemplifying the ethos of the African Dream. They have cultivated a vibrant community of PALs (Pan African Lifestylers) and have disseminated their expertise in social media, marketing, and branding to Afrifluencers worldwide.

Hailing from the Democratic Republic of the Congo, Emmanuel and Solange spent their formative years in

Canada, where they met, married, and embarked on their journey as partners in life and business. With a steadfast commitment to God and family, they transplanted their aspirations to the African soil, establishing the headquarters of Pan African Lifestyle in the motherland.

Emmanuel Bope, an astute business luminary and creative visionary, spearheads PAL as its CEO and co-founder. Armed with a diploma in Public Relations, a diploma in Marketing Communication, and a degree in Marketing Science, he orchestrates PAL's strategic direction with unparalleled acumen.

Solange Bope, a dynamic force of creativity, thrives on innovation and impact, forging emotional connections through brand and narrative. Solange is the President and co-founder of Pan African Lifestyle Inc. With a background as an entrepreneur and fashionista, she infuses PAL's ventures with her flair for style and storytelling. Holding diplomas in Fashion Styling and Image Consulting, as well as Marketing Communications, she brings a unique blend of artistry and business acumen to the PAL ecosystem.

Together, Emmanuel and Solange Bope stand as exemplars of Pan-Africanism, prioritizing the development of the motherland while cherishing their roles as life partners, confidants, and parents. Their unwavering dedication to forging a new narrative for Africa through media underscores their commitment to shaping a brighter future for the continent and its people. Today, the Bopes serve as brand and media consultants, keynote speakers, entrepreneurs, and philanthropist focused on inspiring The African Dream.

www.ingramcontent.com/pod-product-compliance
Lightning Source LLC
Chambersburg PA
CBHW040929210326
41597CB00030B/5235

IN "AFRIFLUENCE," WE EMBARK ON A TRANSFORMATIVE JOURNEY INTO THE HEART OF AFRICAN CREATIVITY, EXPLORING ITS IMMENSE POTENTIAL TO RESHAPE NARRATIVES, PERCEPTIONS, AND ECONOMIES ON A GLOBAL SCALE. THIS BOOK IS MORE THAN JUST A GUIDE—IT'S A MANIFESTO FOR AFRICAN INFLUENCERS READY TO HARNESS THE TRUE POWER OF THEIR CREATIVE CONTENT AND CAPITALIZE ON THE WEALTH OF OPPORTUNITIES AWAITING THEM.

ISBN 978-1-7776963-9-9

90000

9 781777 696399